# REALLY! Maddening MAZES

## A Collection of Pathfinding Puzzles to Frazzle your Nerves

Almost everything we do involves choices. Some decisions are relatively minor and have little bearing on our life as a whole. But many of the choices we make shape who we are and what we will become.

It is not always clear if the paths we have chosen will lead us to the goals we have set. But through the journey we learn and grow and become more skillful at finding our way.

Enjoy these pathfinding puzzles, which echo the routes we select while making our way to the destinations we desire.

Illustrations & Content by
**Rick Jaspers**

**Dover Publications, Inc.**
Mineola, New York

Dedicated to my parents, who prepared me to travel this pathway, to my wife, Kelly, who walks it beside me, and to my two sons, Chris and Andy, who remind me that getting lost and finding my way back can be an awful lot of fun.

*Bibliographical Note*

*Really Maddening Mazes* is a new work, first published by Dover Publications, Inc., in 2012.

*International Standard Book Number*
*ISBN-13: 978-0-486-48278-1*
*ISBN-10: 0-486-48278-2*

Manufactured in the United States by Courier Corporation
48278202    2014
www.doverpublications.com

# Table of Contents

# #1: CHARTRES CATHEDRAL MAZE

A maze similar to the one on the opposite page was constructed on the floor of the Chartres Cathedral in France. Because of the circular design of the cathedral, some people think the fabled Knights Templar were responsible for creating this maze, as well as the church that houses it. Although the original maze has many twists and turns, it is a single path that winds through the entire circle. There are no side paths or dead ends. The path symbolizes the journey through life with all its unexpected turns.

This design is sometimes used as a "meditational finger maze." By following the path with your finger (or a pencil), it is said to have a calming effect. Clear your mind and focus on the labyrinth on the right. Now follow the path from the bottom until it leads you to the center.

Now that you are relaxed, try solving the maze on the opposite page. Enter at the bottom of the maze, and try to find your way into the very center.

Solution appears on page 70

5

# #2: SPIDER WEB MAZE

Spiders play a significant role in controlling insect populations throughout the world. Without them we would feel the impact of more damaged and destroyed crops, a significant rise in diseases transmitted by insect hosts, and just the general annoyance that a large number of "bugs" would bring into our everyday lives.

Spiders are the ultimate environmentally friendly method of pest control. How successful are they? It is estimated that spiders consume nearly 2 billion pounds of insects per day. In fact, they are credited with eating more insects than birds do.

And yet with all the benefits that spiders provide for us, we still tend to see them as creatures to be feared. Maybe it is the fangs and the reputation thrust upon spiders by the handful of species that truly are dangerous to people. Then again it could be the eight eyes, hairy bodies or the way they move. Perhaps it is their skill as successful predators and the unusual ways in which they catch and kill prey that instill fear in us.

Whatever it is, our fear of spiders runs so deep that most everyone knows the word for this fear, arachnophobia. Arachnophobia is one of the most common phobias that people have.

Here are some other common phobias:

**Ophidiophobia:** The fear of snakes        **Acrophobia:** The fear of heights
**Mysophobia:** The fear of germs or dirt   **Claustrophobia:** Fear of confined spaces
**Brontophobia:** The fear of thunderstorms **Nyctophobia:** The fear of the dark

If you were the fly, on the opposite page, you would have reason to fear spiders. Pretend you are the fly and see if you can get out of the web without touching the silk strands. Don't take too many wrong turns, because the spider is on its way!

Solution appears on page 70

# #3: REFLECT ON THIS

For the maze on the opposite page, enter on the left side of the paper. Follow a path which leads out the right side of the paper. Simple enough, right? Wait, there's more. Hold the top edge of the page up to a large mirror.

The path you follow will lead you into the reflected image on the mirror (possibly more than once). How you choose to trace your path on the mirror is up to you. That is part of the challenge.

Oh, and one more thing. Barriers have been placed throughout the maze. When you see a P , that means you can not cross that area while on the paper. The M indicates that the way is blocked if you are on the mirror.

A version of the maze has been place to the right which has the reflected image placed into it. This is for those who have great difficulty with the mirror. It may be much easier, but I guarantee it is not nearly as fun, so give the mirror version a try first.

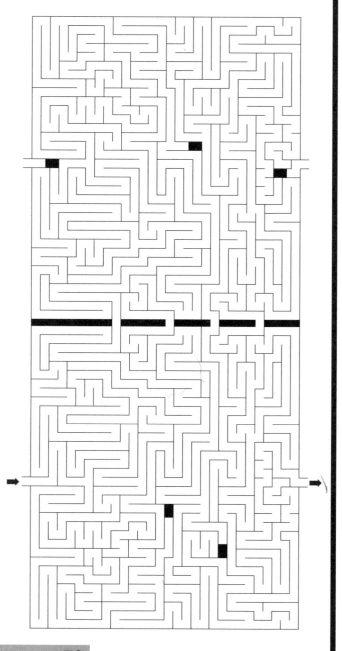

Solution appears on page 70

# #4: WORM MAZE

## Wilbur worm wiggles while we watch

The line above describes what is happening in the maze on the opposite page. Every word starts with a "w". Give the little critter a new name and write a sentence about it with every word starting with the first letter of his new name.

_____

_____

Follow the path from Wilbur's head to the star. When his body moves under or away from the magnifying glass, his size will change. You may cross the edge of the magnifying glass even though it cuts in front of the worm.

---

## Try these two tough tests
You may need a real magnifying glass to do these micro mazes.

**#5 MICRO MAZE 1 (Paramecium)**

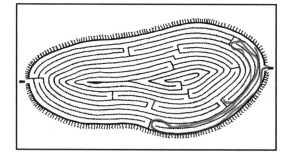

**#6 MICRO MAZE 2 (Amoeba)**

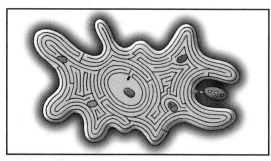

Solutions appear on page 71

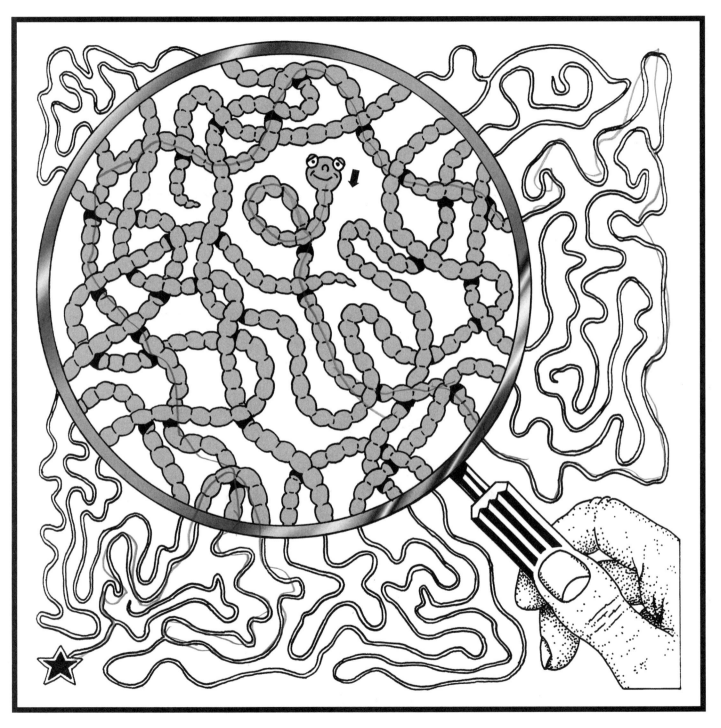

# #7: BAMBOO MAZE

Bamboo is a versatile material due to its fast growth, incredible strength and beauty. Check out some of the facts and uses of this amazing plant.

## Bamboo Facts:

- Bamboo is the fastest growing plant on earth. Reports of record growth range from one to four feet a day for some species.

- Thomas Edison used bamboo as a filament in the world's first incandescent light bulb. The original bulb still burns in the Smithsonian Institute Museum.

- The inventor Alexander Graham Bell used bamboo as the needle for his first phonograph.

Follow the bamboo culm (stem) from where it grows out of the ground, and find your way into the center of the maze, where the leaves are growing.

## The ABCs of Bamboo uses:

**A**-Acupuncture Needles
**B**-Bikes
**C**-Crutches
**D**-Desks
**E**-Edible Shoots
**F**-Fishing Poles
**G**-Garments
**H**-Houses
**I**-Incense Sticks
**J**-Jars
**K**-Knives
**L**-Ladders
**M**-Medicines
**N**-Napkin Rings
**O**-Organ Pipes
**P**-Paper Pulp
**R**-Ropes
**S**-Shingles
**T**-Traps
**U**-Umbrellas
**V**-Vases
**W**-Wheelbarrows
**X**-Xylophones
**Y**-Yarn
**Z**-Zoo Landscaping

Solution appears on page 71

13

# #8: ANT MAZE

Navigating this maze can be tricky. Try to find a path from the opening in the lower left. Squeeze between these ants without bumping into any of them. Some of the gaps are so small that your pencil lead will touch an ant on either side if it is not sharpened to a fine point. To make it through safely, you must exit the opening at the upper right.

---

These ants may all appear the same, as ants usually do, but if you look a bit closer there are some that are different. Can you find the ones listed below?

- ☑ Ant with wings
- ☑ Ant with flag
- ☑ Spider
- ☑ Ant with shoes

- ☑ Ant wearing mittens
- ☑ Ant with ball and chain
- ☐ Ant with eye glasses
- ☑ Ant with ice cream cone

- ☑ Ant with fork
- ☑ Ant blowing bubbles
- ☑ Ants in love

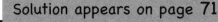
Solution appears on page 71

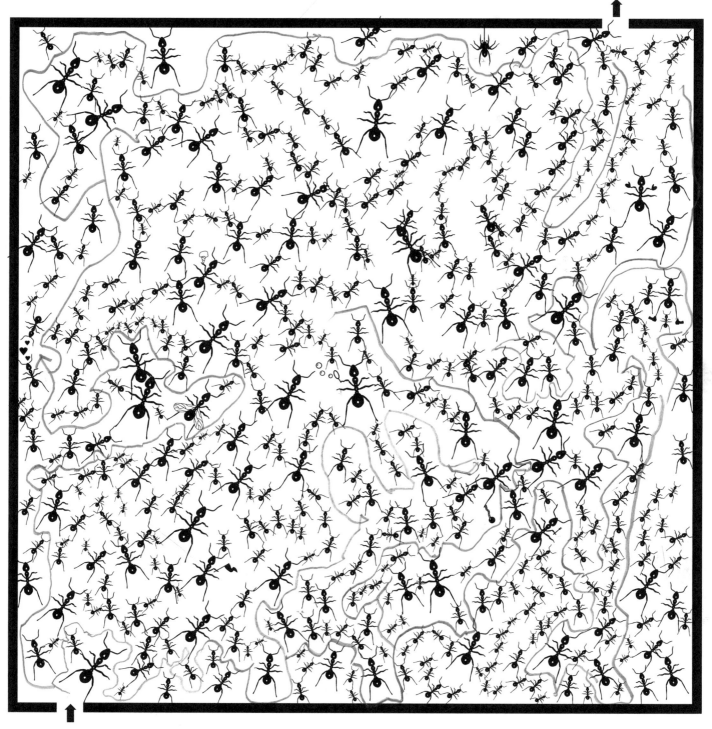

# #9: SWIRLING MAZE

As your pencil touches the paper, you feel a strange sensation as if you are being drawn down into a swirling vortex. You try to pull away, but are overcome by the hypnotic image before you. Your head starts to spin. Fear strikes you. Will you be engulfed by this whirlpool, forever lost in the abyss?

Most likely not; after all this is just a maze. Whoa, you sure do have quite an imagination.

Anyway, to solve this maze, start at the opening at the lower left, and find your way to the center.

---

Obstacles are those frightful things you see when you take your eyes off your goal.  -Henry Ford (Founder of Ford Auto Company)

The road leading to a goal does not separate you from the destination; it is essentially a part of it.  -Charles de Lint (Canadian fantasy author)

---

The inspiration for these mazes was spawned from doodles created while spending endless hours seated in a small guard shack over 32 years ago. The first completed maze was done in 1978 and appears on page 45.

Solution appears on page 72

# #10: ANOTHER MAZE TO THINK ABOUT

The Human Brain. It's not much to look at, but this three pound mass of wrinkled tissue is truly a marvel. Although it only accounts for 2% of an individual's body weight, this extraordinary organ definitely pulls its weight when it comes to performance. Here are some of the things it can do:

• The brain monitors and regulates the involuntary bodily processes, such as heart rate, breathing, body temperature, digestion and hundreds of other systems throughout the body. All without us having to give it a second thought.

• It also houses the control center for higher mental activity including thought, reason and abstract thinking.

• In its role as a communication center, the brain receives information from parts of the body, and then sends signals to other parts. Some of these signals travel at speeds up to 268 mph. That is faster than the top speed of an Indy car.

• Although the brain does not contain receptors for the senses, it does process and interpret the input for sight, hearing, taste, smell and touch, and it decides what to do with that information.

• The brain gives us the ability to make decisions, is responsible for personality, allows us to store memories, and enables us with the capacity for emotion.

As you can see, the human brain manages and controls many different functions. It is the ultimate multitasker. The brain is also capable of helping you solve the maze on the opposite page!

Solution appears on page 72

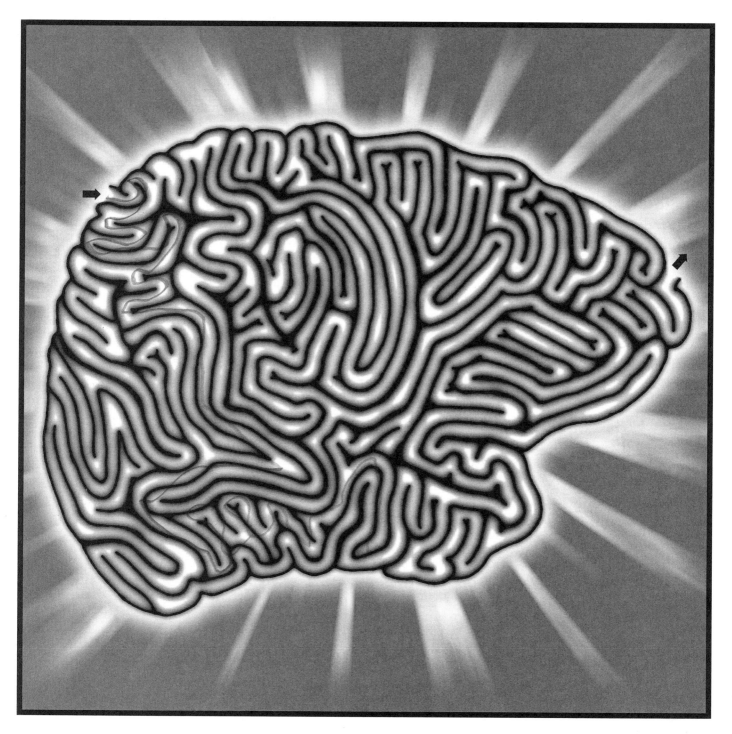

# #11 CORN MAIZE

No, that's not a typo in the title. Another word for corn is maize.

Corn, or maize, is a member of the grass family which is native to North and South America. It was first cultivated by the Mayan, Aztec and Inca Indians over 5,000 years ago.

Though today corn is used primarily as feed for livestock, it has many other culinary uses as well. It can be popped, creamed, boiled, grilled, transformed into a sweetener and made into bread or tortillas. A Brazilian desert known as canjica is made by boiling maize kernels in sweet milk. In Peru, it is made into a soft drink called chicha morada.

Okay—a few mildly interesting facts about corn, but what is the point?

Mazes go back thousands of years, first showing up in the architecture of many parts of the world. Later, garden mazes were developed throughout Europe, incorporating intricate hedges designed for visitors to find the center and then return to the starting point.

A relatively recent step in the evolution of the maze is the "corn maze." Instead of just tracing the solution with a pencil as with the puzzles in this book, you become the "rat", and actually have to find your way through a path carved into a field of corn.

Many of today's corn mazes also feature other attractions including pumpkin patches, hay rides, farmer's markets and petting zoos. Some are even open after dark.

In early fall, keep and eye out for a corn maze in your area, and join in on the fun. Until then, there is always the corn maze on the right to get you by.

Solution appears on page 72

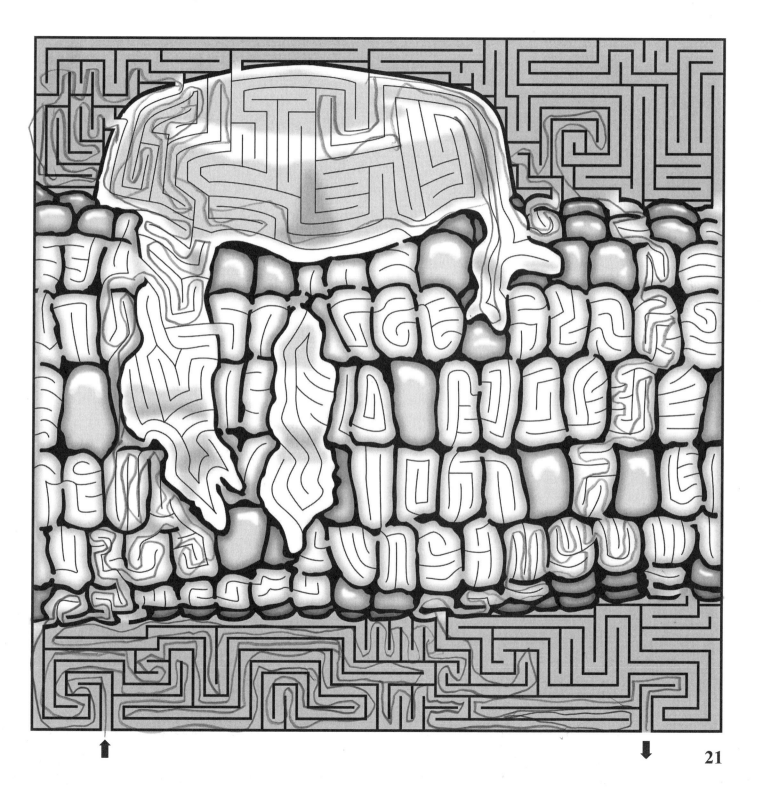

# #12 WHAT IS IT? MAZE

At times, inspiration can come from very strange places. But, in the case of this maze, it is not only inspired by something a bit odd, actually the maze itself is a photograph of this object. Of course it has been doctored up a bit to make it work as a maze.

Would you care to take a guess what it might be? Here are a few clues to get you started:

**CLUE #1:** It is a plant.
**CLUE #2:** It is edible.
**CLUE #3:** It is a vegetable.
**CLUE #4:** It can be eaten raw or cooked.
**CLUE #5:** It is often shredded before it is used.
**CLUE #6:** This type has twice as much Vitamin C as the green variety.
**CLUE #7:** It is often found in coleslaw and salads, but generally not in large amounts.
**CLUE #8:** 1st word— Mars is known as the r e d planet.
**CLUE #9:** 2nd word, 1st syllable— A popular form of travel in New York C A B, add a **B**
**CLUE #10:** 2nd word, 2nd syllable— How old a person is a g e.

Once you have figured out what the mystery object is, try the maze on the opposite page, There is also a recipe below using this secret ingredient.

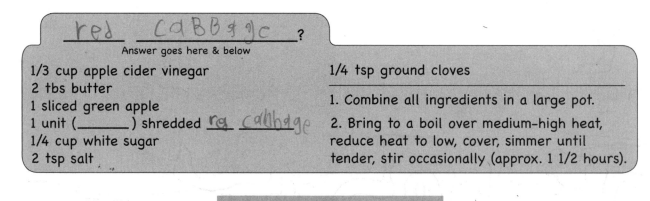

red cabbage ?
Answer goes here & below

1/3 cup apple cider vinegar
2 tbs butter
1 sliced green apple
1 unit (_____) shredded red cabbage
1/4 cup white sugar
2 tsp salt

1/4 tsp ground cloves

1. Combine all ingredients in a large pot.
2. Bring to a boil over medium-high heat, reduce heat to low, cover, simmer until tender, stir occasionally (approx. 1 1/2 hours).

Solution appears on page 72

22

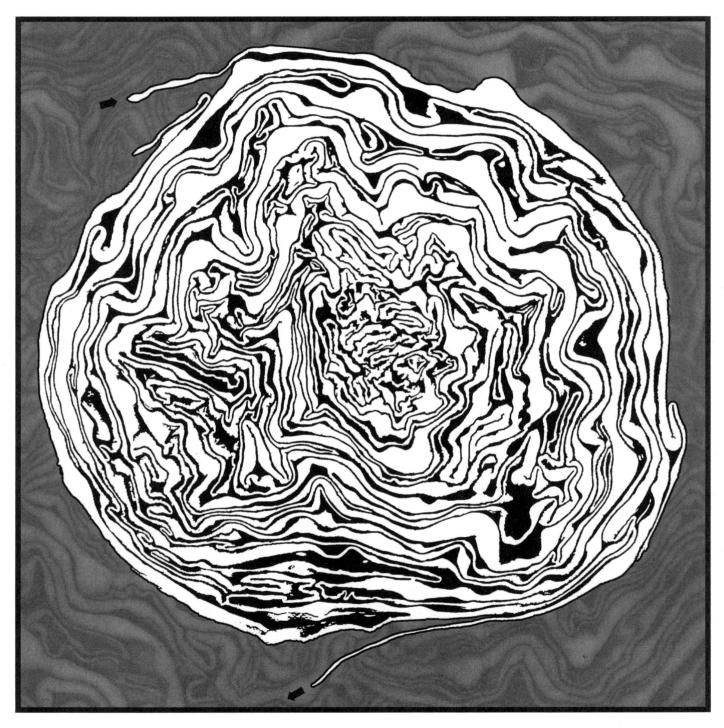

# #13: PENCIL MAZE

Since several pencils have given their lives in the creation of this book, the next two pages have been dedicated to their memory.

Yes we take the lead pencil for granite, but it's not granite at all. In fact it's not lead either. Clay and graphite are used to produce the pencil's center. The pencil is so common, so ordinary, so plain. We chew on it, we bite off its eraser. The lowly pencil gets no respect.

And though we treat it with abuse, the good ole' #2 gives so much back to us. A single pencil can draw a line 34 to 35 miles long and can endure seventeen sharpenings. All that for mere pennies apiece.

So next time you hold the little yellow beauty in your hand, remember to acknowledge the quiet, selfless years of service the pencil has given us.

Most pencils have six sides (hexagon) Why do you think that is? The answer appears below (upside down).

---

Start at the pencil point and move to the eraser.

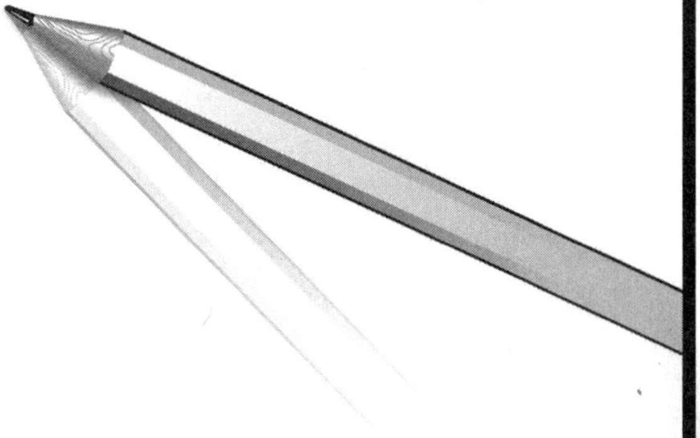

**Answer:** Pencils have six sides to keep them from rolling away off your desk.

Solution appears on page 73

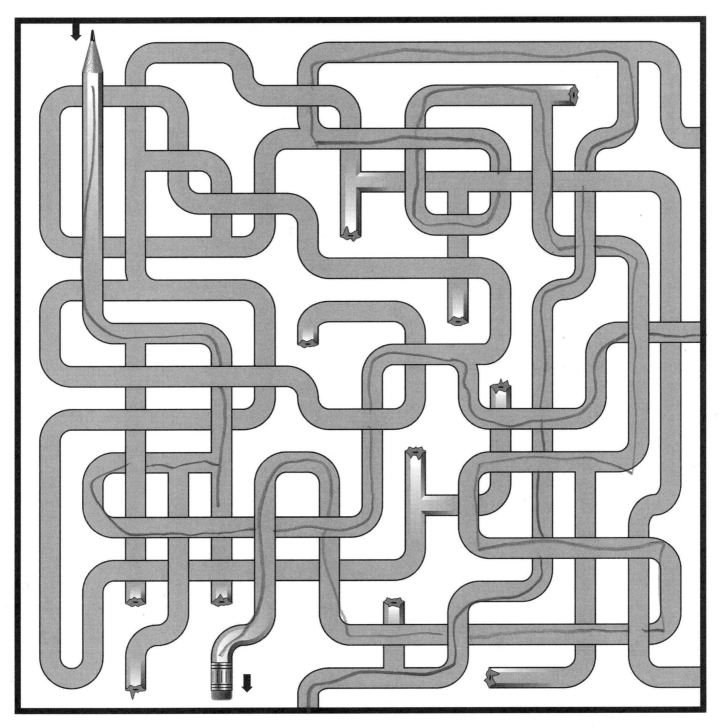

25

# #14 PRAIRIE DOG MAZE

Prairie dogs are burrowing rodents that are closely related to squirrels. Some species of prairie dogs live in scattered burrows, but others form highly social colonies known as "towns." The area of a town may average a half square mile, but some are much bigger. The largest recorded town contained around four hundred million members, and occupied an area of 25,000 square miles. That is roughly the size of 12.1 million football fields (including end zones).

From the burrow entrance, the prairie dog tunnel leads down at a steep angle for around ten feet, where there are specialized chambers used for specific purposes. The bedroom and nursery chambers are lined with dry grass to insulate them from the cold. There are also areas for storage as well as a bathroom. A listening room is located near the entrance, to keep a sharp ear out for predators before going above.

These rabbit-sized rodents feed on grasses, roots, seeds and the occasional insect during the daylight hours. They get all of their water from the food they eat. The mound of dirt piled at the entrance serves as a sentry post, where a guard watches for any danger. If a predator is spotted the guard gives a high pitch warning yelp which sends the prairie dogs scurrying for the safety of the tunnels.

It is thought by some that the prairie dogs possess sophisticated vocalizations which are able to identify several predators including snakes, badgers coyotes, eagles and owls. There is even a sound used to indicate that the danger is gone.

Prairie dogs hibernate during the winter, and survive by burning the fat reserves they have stored up during the rest of the year.

See if you can lead the prairie dog on the opposite page down into the tunnels, and to the sleeping chamber at the bottom of the page.

Solution appears on page 73

# #15: PIPES & GLASS MAZE

Why pipes and glass? Why not? Start at the A (or Alpha in Greek) in the upper left corner. As you proceed along the pipes, you may cross through the glass sheets even though there are barrier lines, but you can not jump from one pipe to another where one appears to pass in front of another. The goal is to reach the symbol in the lower right corner, which is Omega, the last letter of the Greek alphabet.

Greek was the first alphabet that gave a separate symbol to each consonant and vowel. In English the word "alphabet" is derived from the first two letters in Greek, Alpha and Beta.

The English phrase "It's all Greek to me", is often used to indicate something is incomprehensible. But before you think Greek is especially difficult to understand, consider these other roughly translated phrases from around the world that also express the frustration of unfamiliar languages:

- Arabic: Am I speaking Hindi?
- Bulgarian: You're speaking to me in Patagonian!
- Croatian, Czech, Macedonian, Slovak, Slovenian: It's a Spanish village to me.
- Dutch: That's Latin for me.
- Finnish, French: It's all Hebrew to me.
- French: To me it's Javanese.
- German, French, Greek, Hebrew, Hungarian, Lithuanian: That's all Chinese to me.
- Greek, Italian: It's Arabic (to me)

As you can see, language can be quite a barrier to understanding people of other languages and cultures. The fact is, if we could get past the language barriers, we would see that we have much more in common then we think.

Solution appears on page 73

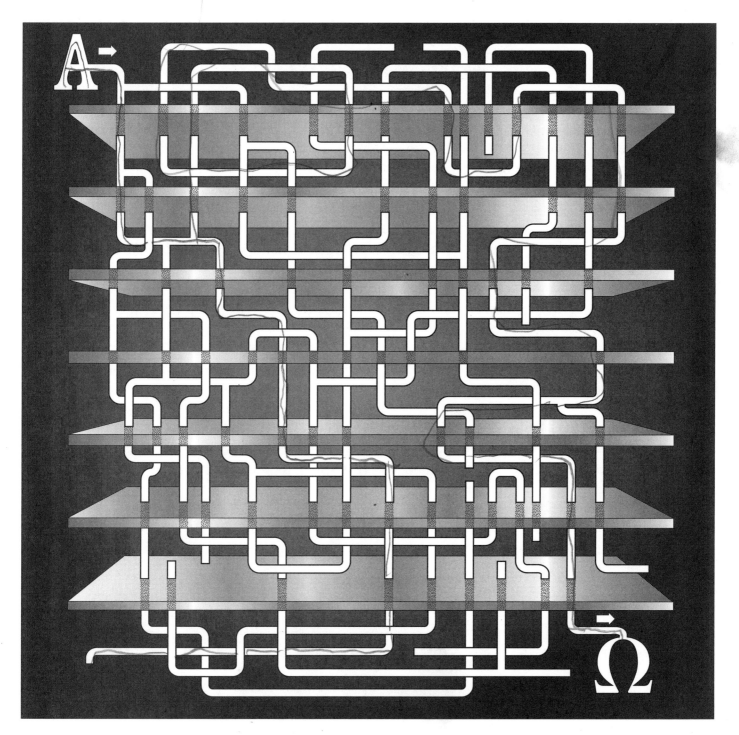

# #16: RAT MAZE

For almost a hundred years, scientists have studied the rodent's ability to solve mazes. Because many rats make their homes in a network of underground tunnels, they are well suited for the task.

One aspect of the rat's progress that is monitored is its memory. By keeping track of the time it takes for the rat to navigate to the finish, and then comparing it to additional runs, we can get a sense of how much memory plays a part in getting to the end. If the time it takes goes down with each attempt, there is a good chance that memory is aiding the rat's ability to solve the maze.

There is also a way to test your maze running skills, and see how memory can help you get though a labyrinth.

First, keep track of how much time it takes you to solve the maze on the opposite page. There is a space to write the time below. You will have to use only your finger to guide you. No pencils allowed.

Now, put the maze aside for a period of time. It could be 1 hour or one day. It is up to you. Remember, in this experiment, you are not only the rat, but also the scientist.

Do the maze as before and write down the results. Run the maze two more times after taking the time break so you have a good sample to analyze.

1st run time ___106 sec.___      2nd run time ___41 sec.___

3rd run time _____      4th run time _____

What can you conclude from the results above? Did memory help you? Don't be alarmed if you are craving a tasty wedge of cheese about now.

Solution appears on page 73

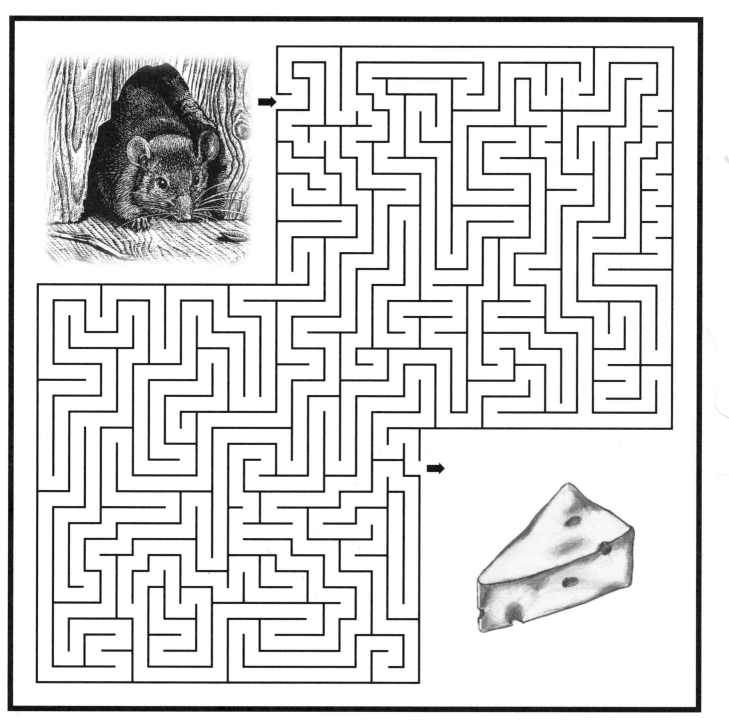

# #17, #18, #19, #20: PHRASE MAZE

This is perhaps the most difficult maze of the bunch. Start from one of the bold consonant letters in the upper left which spell out the word **PROCEED (P, R, C or D).** Try to find a phrase that extends from this letter and is completed in one of the bold letters in the right column (**THE END**).

To find a phrase, movement can be made up, down, left, right, and diagonally any number of spaces before changing directions. No individual letter can be used more than once, and no part of the path may cross over itself for a particular phrase. You may use additional bold letters as you spell out the phrase.

There are a total of 4 paths to discover, one for each of the consonants **(P, R, C or D),** and all of them are completed in the letters which spell out **THE END** in bold.

It will require persistence to solve these mazes. But don't get frustrated if you can't get them right away. Clues have been provided to make the task easier. The phrases are also listed if you have difficulties. Even after you know the phrase, it may be a challenge to find the path.

Solutions appear on page 74, clues & phrases are on page 75

# #21 BONUS PHRASE:

For those who met the challenge of finding the 4 phrases above, there is another quote hidden among the letters in the grid. This phrase starts from one of the bold consonants in the upper left like the others, but it does not end in the bold letters in the right column. Find it if you dare. A clue and the phrase itself are listed with the others if you have troubles.

Solution appears on page 76, clue & phrase are on page 75

| P | R | O | C | E | E | D | R | I | K | I | N | T | H |
|---|---|---|---|---|---|---|---|---|---|---|---|---|---|
| E | A | N | T | S | D | M | E | S | N | L | O | B | R |
| R | E | I | S | N | U | R | N | A | I | H | C | N | I |
| E | S | A | T | O | N | T | S | M | T | E | S | E | V |
| T | N | E | Y | M | O | H | O | F | T | G | R | F | A |
| H | T | N | C | E | C | A | V | B | E | U | R | O | F |
| E | D | R | U | A | R | E | A | N | O | A | O | E | O |
| P | R | I | N | G | T | I | S | F | R | M | Y | A | T |
| E | P | I | N | H | N | M | N | I | E | D | N | S | H |
| F | P | S | O | O | D | A | U | L | E | T | O | N | E |
| E | H | N | U | L | L | O | G | O | S | F | W | N |   |
| T | H | W | E | F | I | H | W | I | U | A | N | I | E |
| I | G | H | O | N | N | A | T | S | O | T | E | L | N |
| E | W | N | A | C | E | S | A | C | A | N | S | E | D |

33

# #22: SPHERES & RODS MAZE

Getting from point A to point B. That is essentially the goal of solving a maze. But let's take a deeper look at what a maze is and what it takes to solve it.

With very few exceptions, the mazes in this book are of a kind known as "standard" or "perfect," which means no path will loop around to somewhere you have already been. Any path you are on will lead to the solution if it does not dead end. If you do reach a dead end, you will have to retrace your path back to a junction, and try a direction you have not yet explored.

This is why using a pencil is helpful. Otherwise you may find yourself retracing your steps clear back to the beginning.

Another idea is to hold or lightly tape a clear plastic sheet over a maze, and solve it with a dry erase pen. Then others can test their skills on the maze as well. This will also allow you to use any of the mazes in this book as additional memory experiments on yourself or others, as described on page 30.

What makes a maze hard or easy? There are several factors that determine the difficulty of a particular maze. Here are a few:

• The length of the solution paths
• The quantity and length of the dead ends
• The amount of turns and twists designed to slow you down
• The skill of the maze designer to lead you on false trails

For the maze on the opposite page, start at the large sphere in the lower left. Follow the rods along from sphere to sphere until you get to the other large sphere in the upper right.

Solution appears on page 76

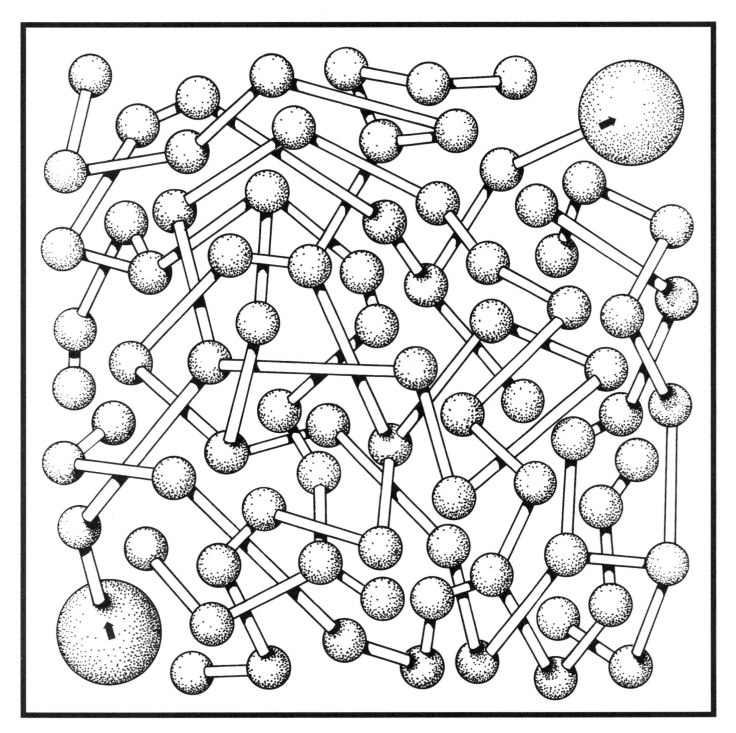

# #23 CREATURE MAZE

The creature floats toward you. This hideous gas-filled blob uses a sail on its back to sneak closer. Its enormous tentacles (some as long as 4 school buses) reach out to grab you. If you are captured, the gruesome beast will ensnare you with its deadly stinging tentacles. These arms will then draw you up to its waiting polyps which will dissolve you with enzymes they produce. This bizarre specter hides a deep secret. It is not actually a single animal at all. It is really a colony of four different types of creatures which depend on one another to survive. You are a small fish and the monster hunting you is the Man-of-War, a jellyfish which lives on the surface of tropical marine waters.

---

Find which tentacle has you in its clutches. Following each tentacle from the body to the end is the only way to escape from being the Man-of-War's next victim. Good Luck!

Solution appears on page 76

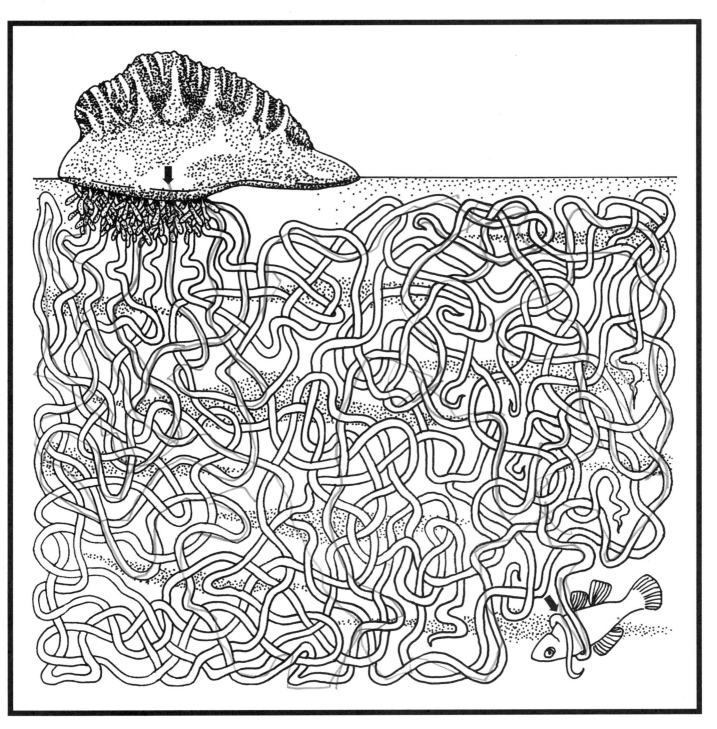

# #24 PRETZEL MAZE

The shape of the pretzel was developed a long time ago by a monk in Europe. He used the left over ends of dough from bread making. The monk formed strips of dough to represent children's arms folded in prayer. He would give these twisted loops to young ones who did well learning their prayers. He called his creation a pretiola which is Latin for "little reward." Over the years the name became a symbol of excellence in accomplishment.

---

Lennie owned a bakery. One day his pretzel maker went home sick. Several customers came in to buy pretzels, but there were none. Lennie started to think of all the business he was losing because he had no pretzels. "How hard could it be," he thought to himself. Lennie decided that he was going to make the pretzels. He first mixed the ingredients and rolled out the dough. He was very good at making bread so this part was easy. But looping the dough into the right shape turned out to be much harder. The more he tried, the more frustrated he became. Finally he made a pretzel which he thought looked pretty good, so he put it in the oven. The pretzel he made is on the opposite page. What do you think? Does Lennie deserve a pretiola?

Can you find a way to get from the end of the pretzel on the left side to the end on the right?

Solution appears on page 76

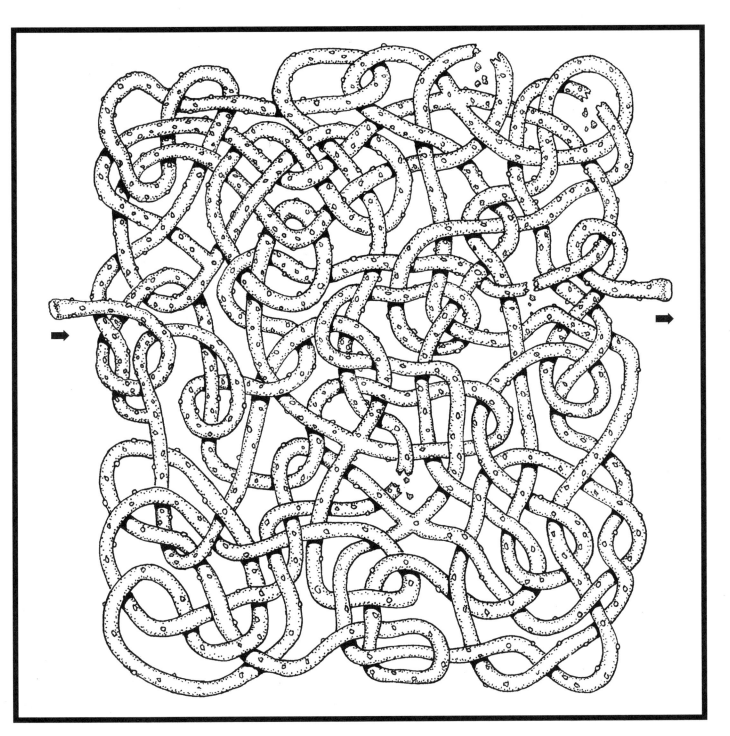

39

# #25: TREASURE MAZE

Ahoy landlubber,

So ye be fixin' to rid me of me treasure, says you.

Tis a nice tide t' sail, and the wind be at yer aft, says I.

But before ye cast off matey, be warned. Untold perils await those that sail these waters.

Oh, and one more thing. Thar be talk o' a monster that lurks in the depths. Take me word, it be more than chat from those that be swabin' the decks too long.

I have seen this vile creature with me one good eye when I buried the treasure, and barely escaped to tell the tale.

Shiver me timbers! Ye still be riskin' a trip to Davey Jones locker for a chest of gold doubloons?

Very well, me hearty. If ye be set on this folly, navigate your ship with great care. Using the treasure map, follow the dotted lines to guide you to the chest.

Solution appears on page 77

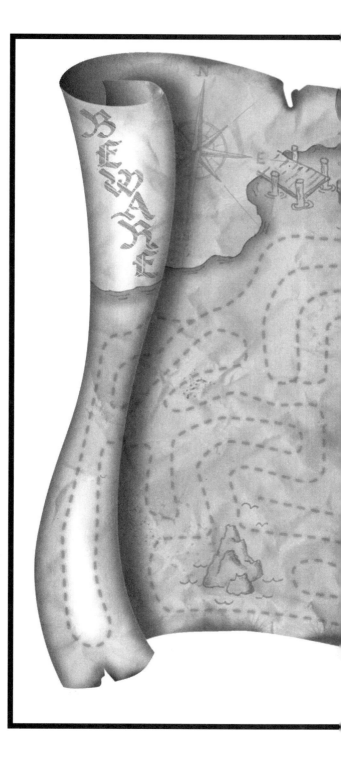

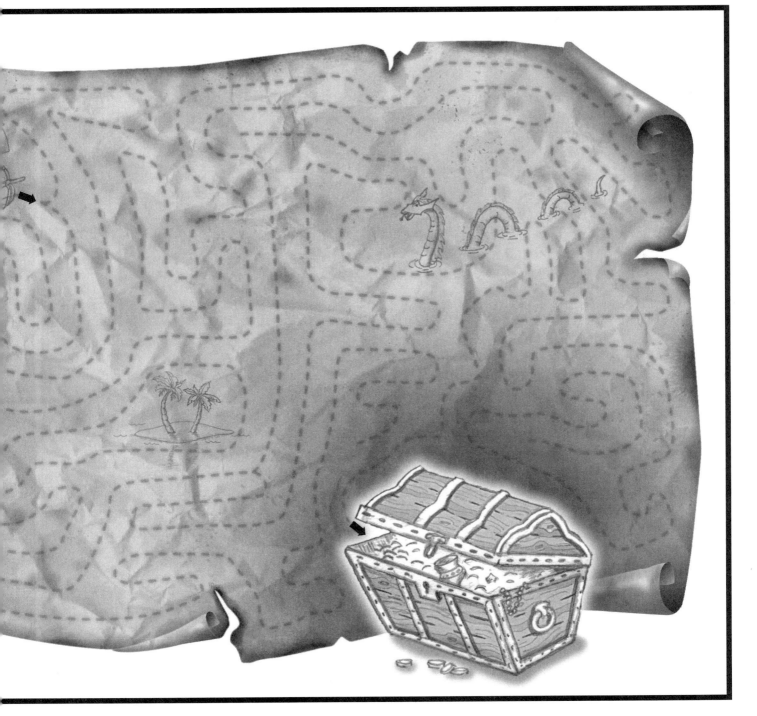

# #26: IVY MAZE

Ivy is a popular ornamental plant widely used as a ground cover. This evergreen rapidly carpets an area, and maintains a height of under a foot.

Since ivy thrives in full shade to full sun and grows well in most soil types, it is considered extremely hardy. Used as a ground cover it is helpful in reducing erosion.

Another widespread use of ivy is as a climbing plant. It can be found on many architectural exterior walls, particularly brick buildings as well as ornamental structures such as trellises.

English ivy produces two types of leaves.

The lobed juvenile leaves grow close to the ground on thin tendril like stems, but will climb any objects which they come in contact with. The leaves are dark green and shiny with light green veins

The adult leaves grow high into the crowns of the trees where they are exposed to the sunlight. These leaves have stems which are woody and can reach several inches in diameter. The adult plants produce pale yellow flowers, and a purple fruit that is eaten by many species of birds, which can carry the seeds off to be propagated elsewhere.

In many areas, ivy is considered a nuisance, and can be difficult to control once it takes hold in a natural habitat.

To solve the maze on the opposite page, start at the hanging planter. Follow the main branch which grows out of it. Your goal is to follow the ivy stems to the ladybug in the lower right corner.

Solution appears on page 77

43

# #27: HOSE MAZE

Water. It's everywhere. We've all heard the facts. It covers 70 to 75% of the earth's surface. Almost 60% of the human body is water. Pretty impressive numbers. And on top of that, water is able to regenerate itself by evaporation, and is redistributed in the form of rain and snow. It appears to be endless.

But let's take a closer look at water. Although it is hard to deny the abundance of water, 97% of the world's water is salty and undrinkable. Add to this another 2% that is frozen in glaciers and polar ice caps. So we are only left with 1%. Remember, we need to share this with the plants and animals of the world, which also depend on water.

So now this liquid substance takes on a greater importance as a precious commodity. Maybe not quite as valuable as gold or silver, but then again, we can live without gold. Aside from air, water is the most necessary substances for our survival.

There are many ways to conserve water, way too many to mention here. Since, in some areas, over half the residential water is used for outdoor watering, let's just look at the hose and a couple quick conservation tips:

• Use a broom to clean sidewalks and driveways instead of a hose to save 150 gal.
• A drippy hose can lose up to 2,150 gal. a year.
• Often, a leak can be fixed by replacing a washer or wrench tightening the hose.
• Wash cars with a pail of soapy water, and use a hose with a nozzle for rinsing.

Start there and discover new ways of your own to conserve water.

Begin at the faucet, and follow the hose to discover which way leads to the bucket. It looks like the hose has sprung a leak, so try not to get wet.

Solution appears on page 77

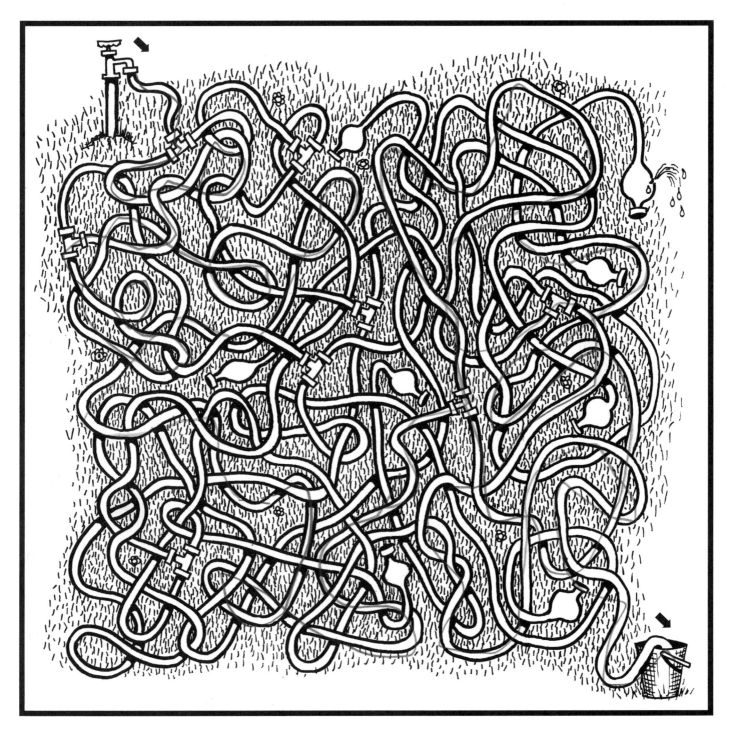

45

# #28: LEAF MAZE

Did you know the thing which makes leaves green is called chlorophyll? It enables a tree to change water and carbon dioxide into oxygen and a kind of sugar called glucose, using the energy from sunlight. The glucose is food for the tree. This process is called photosynthesis. We breathe oxygen produced by the trees and other plants. When we breathe out, the oxygen is changed back into carbon dioxide, to be used again by the plants.

Why do leaves change colors? It all goes back to the chlorophyll. During the growing season, chlorophyll is produced in abundance to produce food. But as summer comes to an end, the trees prepare for winter. As the trees shut down their food making factories in the leaves, the green chlorophyll disappears. Other pigments that have been hidden by the green in the leaves now start to show through.

After a brief show of brilliant colors, the leaves undergo another change. This change is reflected by the name of the season in which it happens, Fall. It is commonly thought that wind or frost triggers the trees to shed their leaves. But the truth is that the trees themselves bring about this change. Some types of leaves are not able to withstand freezing temperatures, so the trees must discard them each year, and grow new ones the following season.

When the leaves fall, they are not wasted. They decompose, and become a nutrient rich layer of the forest floor.

---

Follow the path up the stem and go to the place at the top of the page where oxygen is being released.

Solution appears on page 78

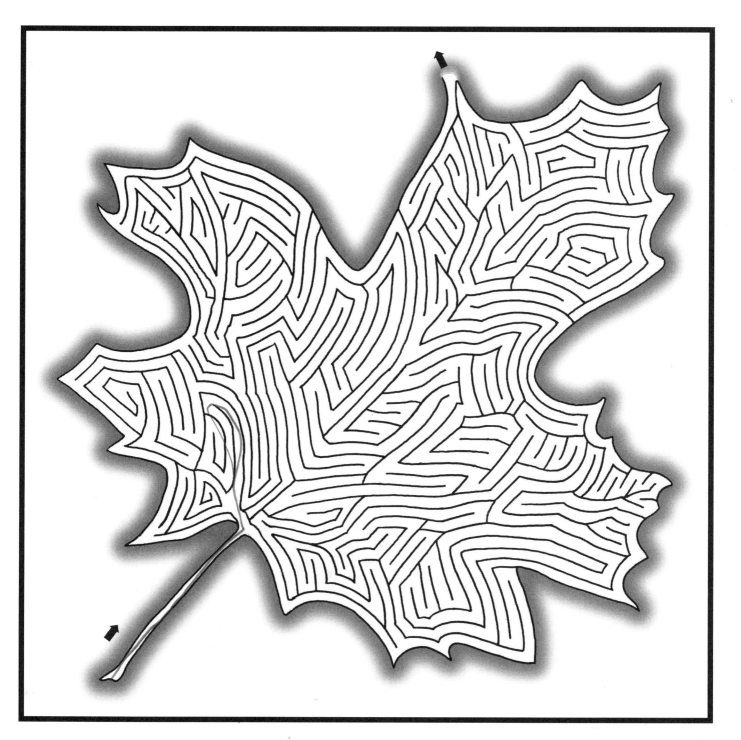

47

# #29: MUSICAL MAZE

How would you like to create a musical symphony using glass soda bottles? Okay, symphony might be a little optimistic, but creating music should be realistic enough.

First, you will need 4 empty glass soda bottles, some water and a spoon. Fill as indicated by the group of 4 the gray bottles you see here. Arrange as shown.

Now gently tap each with the spoon. What do you notice about the relationship of the water level to the pitch of the sound? Yes, the higher the volume, the lower the note.

Try using your spoon to play "Mary had a Little Lamb" using the guide below:

B A G A B B B A A A B D D B A G A B B B B A A B A G

Ready for something new? Add water to the bottle with the least amount until it looks like the gray one by itself. Blow across the open lip of one of the bottles. Can you make it whistle? You may have to practice a little. It can be tricky. Now try another. Did you notice that it works differently than with the spoon. A higher volume creates a higher note.

Play the song below by blowing into the bottles. Does this tune sound familiar?

B A G A B B B A A A B D D B A G A B B B B A A B A G

To solve this Seussian maze, start at the arrow on the left, and follow the pipes. See if you can find where the sound is coming out.

Solution appears on page 78

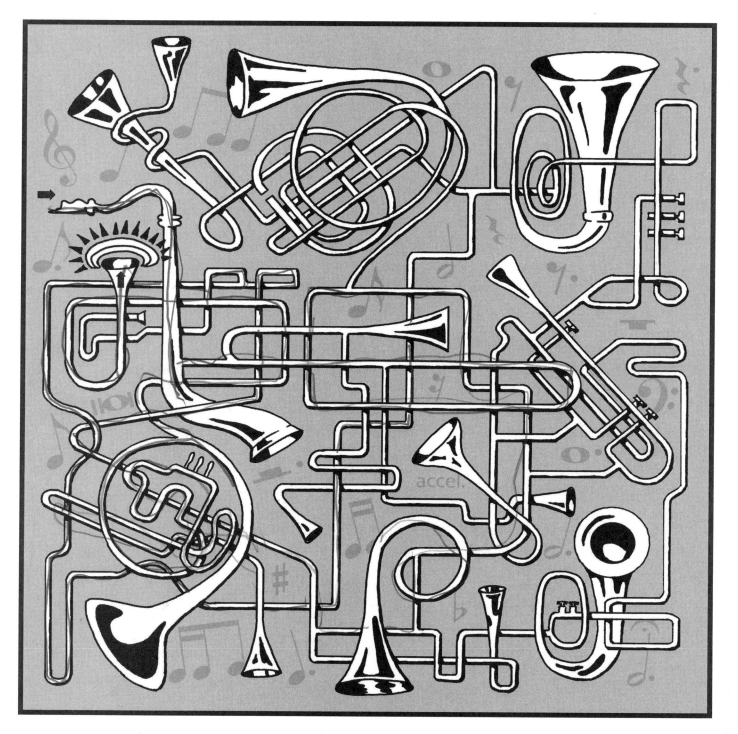

# #30: DANDELION MAZE

The dreaded dandelion is the scourge of gardeners the world over. Dandelions reek havoc in lawns, gardens and flower beds. They truly are a weed in every sense of the word.

And yet these magnificent plants seem to have an enchanting quality to them as well. One day they are hidden from sight, and the next they bring forth a spectacular display of yellow flowers.

But these hollow stemmed plants are not yet done captivating us. Suddenly, as if by magic, the flowers are transformed into globes of delicate white so beautiful, they rival the flowers they replaced.

Each ball is made up of hundreds of tiny stalks with a group of hairs on one end. Soon, with some encouragement by the wind, these miniature parachutes take to the sky, allowing their cargo to travel great distances.

When the time is right, a single seed drops to the ground, and begins to produce a dandelion plant of its own.

Try to complete the dandelion maze on the opposite page. There is also a kids activity to the right telling how to make your own parachute.

## How to Make a Parachute:

1. Cut a square of plastic wrap.
2. Reinforce each corner with a piece of tape
3. Poke a small hole in each piece of tape
4. Tie one end of equal length thread through each hole.
5. Tie the other ends together on a small weight or a paper clip.

Solution appears on page 78

51

# #31 CHESS MAZE

Chess is known as the game of kings due to the fact that for many centuries it was primarily played by the upper classes and nobility. Today it is the game of choice for many intellectuals. Experienced players are able to see several moves ahead while they plot their strategies.

But for those of us not possessing noble blood or intellectual prowess, chess can still be enjoyable and challenging if pared with an opponent somewhere near our own skill level.

Here is a quick look at the pieces and their abilities:

**Pawn**: Each player has 8 pawns. A pawn can move two spaces forward from its starting position, but only one space forward after that. While capturing an opponent's piece the pawn must move diagonally forward one space.

**Knight**: This piece is the only piece with the ability to jump over other pieces. It can move from one corner to the other of any 2x3 rectangle of squares.

**Bishop**: A Bishop can only move diagonally forwards or backwards.

**Rook**: Movement is made either horizontally or vertically.

**Queen**: The queen may move in any direction.

**King**: The king must be guarded at all costs. If the king is captured the game is over and your opponent wins. It can move one space any direction.

---

For the maze to the right, find the path of moves for the white queen to put the black king in check mate.

Solution appears on page 78

# #32: GOLF MAZE

Have you ever played golf? Interested in playing a game of maze golf? Here's how it works. Keep track of the number of balls you encounter at dead ends as you attempt to get your ball into the cup. When you come to a dead end, backtrack to an intersection and try another route. Add the ball at the beginning to your total, and that is your score. To make it more interesting you can challenge someone else to a game and see who can get the lowest score. But if you do, you will need to use your finger to trace the path, not a pencil.

Since the difficulty level of individual golfing fairways varies, the term "par" is used to indicate the number of strokes an expert golfer is expected to tally to complete a particular hole.

**Here is how to rate your game:**

1 ball: Hole-in-one, double eagle (3 under par), amazing!!!

2 to 5 balls: Eagle (2 under par)

6 to 9 balls: Birdie (1 under par)

10 to 13 balls: Par

14 to 17 balls: Bogey (1 over par)

18 to 21 balls: Double bogey

22 to 25 balls: Triple bogey

Solution appears on page 79

# #33: A THORNY MAZE

Start at the dirt in the lower right. Proceed up the stem until you come to the rose.

_____

Below are some other common flowers. However, the letters are scrambled to form other words. Can you put the letters back together so they spell the flowers again. When solving, remember that the spaces in these anagrams do not appear in the original words (all of the flower names are only one word long). The answers appear on page 79.

Red navel _____       Angry head _____

Image run _____       Sire wait _____

Even bar _____        Grandpa son _____

Old gas rim _____     Fold if sad _____

Mantis pie _____      Any hitch _____

Ape unit _____        List up _____

Dodo horn nerd_____   Nose pie _____

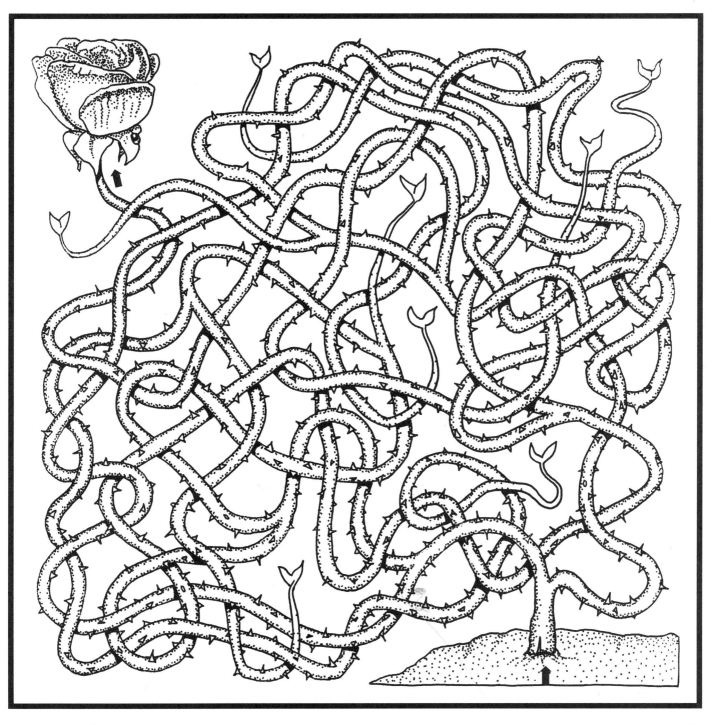

# #34: FINGERPRINT MAZE

Just as each snowflake is different and unique, so too is every person. We all have our own individuality. Fingerprints remind us of these differences which make each of us special. No two people or fingerprints are the same.

Make your own set of fingerprints in the chart below. One at a time, roll each finger on a washable ink pad from fingernail to fingernail. Then roll them again in the proper place of the chart. You may want to try it on scrap paper first to see if you are using the right amount of ink. If you use a light touch, the valleys (white lines) as well as the ridges will be visible, and it should look similar to the graphic on the opposite page, only smaller. Look carefully at each fingerprint. Can you see what features make them unique?

|  | Thumb | Pointer | Middle | Ring | Pinky |
|---|---|---|---|---|---|
| **RIGHT** |  |  |  |  |  |
| **LEFT** |  |  |  |  |  |

On the right is an enlarged fingerprint that has been turned into a maze. From the outside, try to find the white trail that will take you to the star in the middle.

NAME

Solution appears on page 79

59

# #35 TREE RINGS

The maze on page 63 shows a recently cut tree trunk. We can tell many things about a tree and its history by looking at the growth rings on the trunk. The Study of these rings is called Dendrochronology.

Each year a tree produces a new ring. The ring from the first year is the dot in the center. Every dark band represents another year. The outer band is the year the tree was cut.

Take a close look at the rings. If you count the dark rings, you can determine things about its history. How many years did this tree live (A)_____?

In years that the tree had good growing conditions, such as plenty of rain and sunlight, the rings grew far apart. When there was not enough rainfall or temperatures were particularly cold, the rings were tightly packed. Try to find years with an abundance of rain and years of little rain.

See if you can find a year which might indicate damage from fire. It will appear as a dark area along a ring. How long ago was the damage done (B)_____?

On the line below write down an event from your own life and draw a line to where it would be on the tree rings to the right.

_____

Start at the center of the maze on the opposite page and find your way out.

Solution and answers appear on page 80

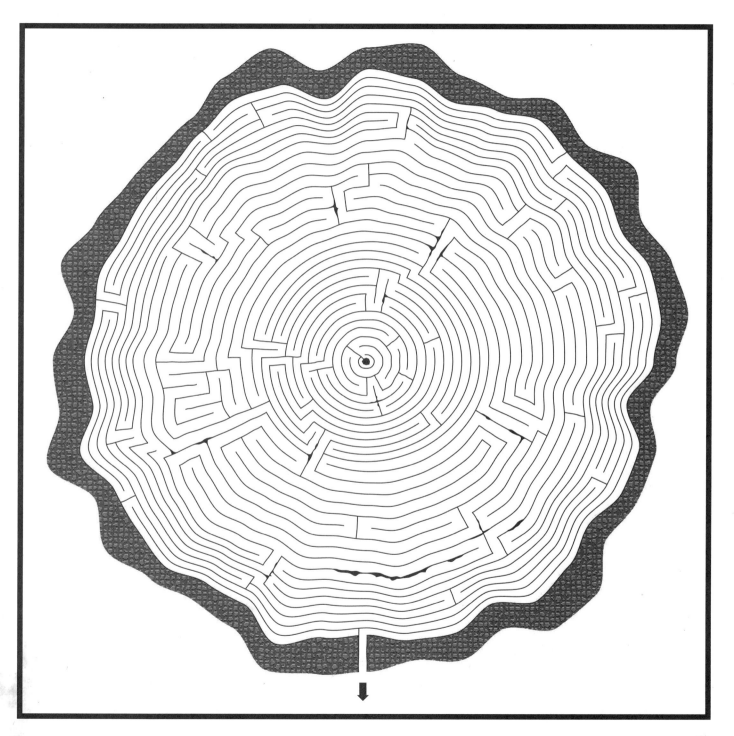

# #36: ROMAN TILE MOSAIC MAZE

The Romans built many wonderful mosaic tile mazes. They were generally designed in a square pattern, and consisted of a single path with no offshoots (unicursal). Although we often use the words "maze" and "labyrinth" to mean the same thing, a more precise definition would make a distinction that a labyrinth is designed only using a single path. A maze can have offshoots and dead ends. This means that all labyrinths are mazes, but not all mazes are labyrinths.

The Roman labyrinths were divided into four quarters. One section was entered and finished before moving into another section. The four quarters of the maze looked the same but were assembled using rotational symmetry by pivoting each section 90 degrees to the one next to it.

The maze on the right was based upon classic Roman tile patterns. The paths were manipulated to create a maze with alternate paths to get lost in.

Enter through the white tile path on the right side of the maze. The goal is the center rectangle.

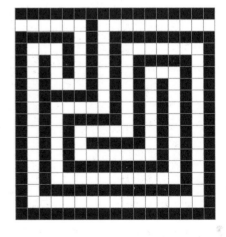

**Which path is unicursal?** Look at the two white paths on either side of this text. They may look the same, but two tiles have switched colors. Can you tell which one is a labyrinth (unicursal), and which one is not. If you have any trouble, reread the first paragraph above.

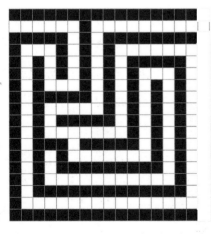

Solution appears on page 80

# #37: TELEPORTATION MAZE

Imagine having your molecules deconstructed, transmitted to another location, and then reassembled again. This may sound a little strange, but it is a widely used method of transportation in science fiction and fantasy. This concept is known as teleportation.

While navigating the maze on the right, you may experience teleportation for yourself, but only if you have a good imagination.

Use the control panel below to see where you are to begin, and how to proceed. Each glass covered transport chamber is imprinted with a symbol. When you reach a transport chamber, the key below will show you where you will transport to next. The chambers are connected with a flexible tube which will either lead you into or out of a maze segment.

Three of the maze segments contain remote transports, which are designated with symbols. If you reach any of these symbols, you will be taken back to the chamber connected to the beginning of the previous maze segment. Now you must go through the segment again, but do not follow the same path as before, or you will find yourself starting the segment once again. There are also dead ends without remote transport symbols. If you reach any, you must retrace your path within the maze segment, and find a way out.

If all goes well, you will end up in the transport chamber marked with three symbols.

May you have a long life and do well.

**START | END**

**REMOTE TRANSPORTS**

**TRANSPORT CHAMBERS**

Solution appears on page 80

# #38: UNDERGROUND PATH MAZE

While gathering food, this poor little ant has lost his way. Can you help him find the path that will take him back to his friends? If you can lead him down from the trail at the top of the maze to the bottom, the ant should be able to pick up the scent of his colony and rejoin the others back on page 15.

Ants are amazing creatures! They are social insects that live in structured communities known as colonies. There are around 10,000 different types of ants. Most varieties live underground, but some make their homes in trees, build mounds above ground, or live in rotten wood.

Although each type of ant colony is organized a little differently, each member has a specific job to do that is important to keep the group strong, safe and healthy.

Another thing ants are known for besides hard work is their strength. They can lift and carry objects 20 times their own body weight. That would be like a person lifting a pick-up truck.

Ant colonies can also be very large. An ant colony can have thousands of members.

So even though ants are very small, they are able to get a lot of work done since they are strong, numerous and hardworking.

---

The more intensely we feel about an idea or a goal, the
more assuredly the idea, buried deep in our subconscious,
will direct us along the path to its fulfillment.
-Earl Nightingale

Solution appears on page 80

# CREATE-A-MAZE

Now that you have solved a few mazes, lets try something new. It is your turn to design a maze for someone else to try.

Before you begin, it might be a good idea to make several copies of the grid to the right so you can create more than one maze.

In almost any maze, you will find five basic elements: A starting point, a goal, walls, gates (any open area that allows you to pass by) and dead ends.

Remember, this is your maze, so you make the rules.

Here are some guidelines to get you started:

• First, decide on a starting point. The easiest way to do this is to draw a box around the outside of the grid leaving a single gap as your starting point. You can pick a finishing point at the beginning, or wait and see how things evolve.

• Trace over sections of the grid to create a path from the beginning point. Create gaps along the way, making paths which lead to dead ends. Include many twists and turns to make the maze more of a challenge. Make sure there is only one path which leads to the finishing point, and that no paths double back onto other paths. Be sure to identify the starting and finishing points. If you have difficulties see how the maze on page 63 is constructed.

• To make a maze which takes less time to build, and is easier to solve, use only the diamond shapes as corner and end points. This will make the paths twice as wide, and less complicated. Another way to make a quicker maze is to only use a portion of the gridded area for your maze. Good luck!

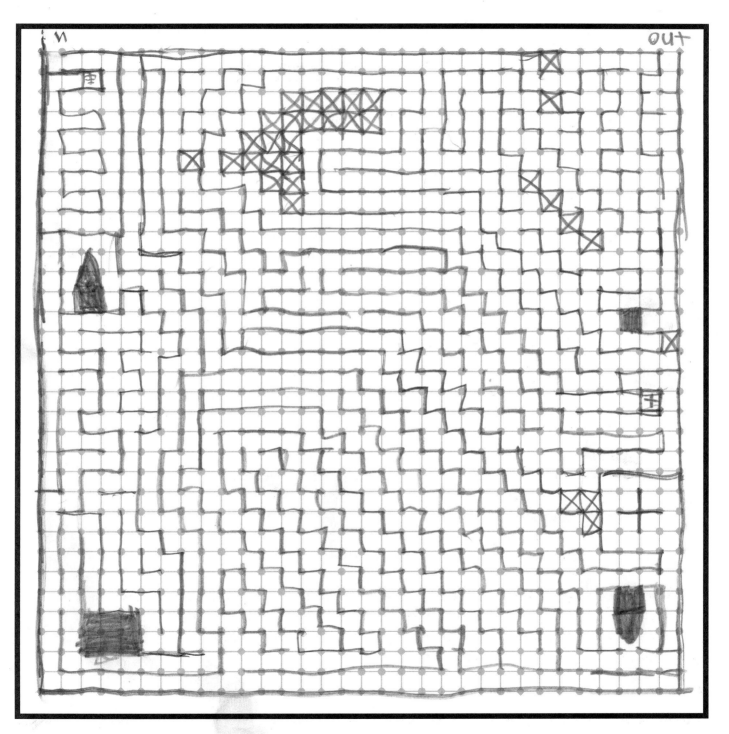

# SOLUTIONS

## #1: CHARTRES CATHEDRAL MAZE

## #3: REFLECT ON THIS

## #2: SPIDER WEB MAZE

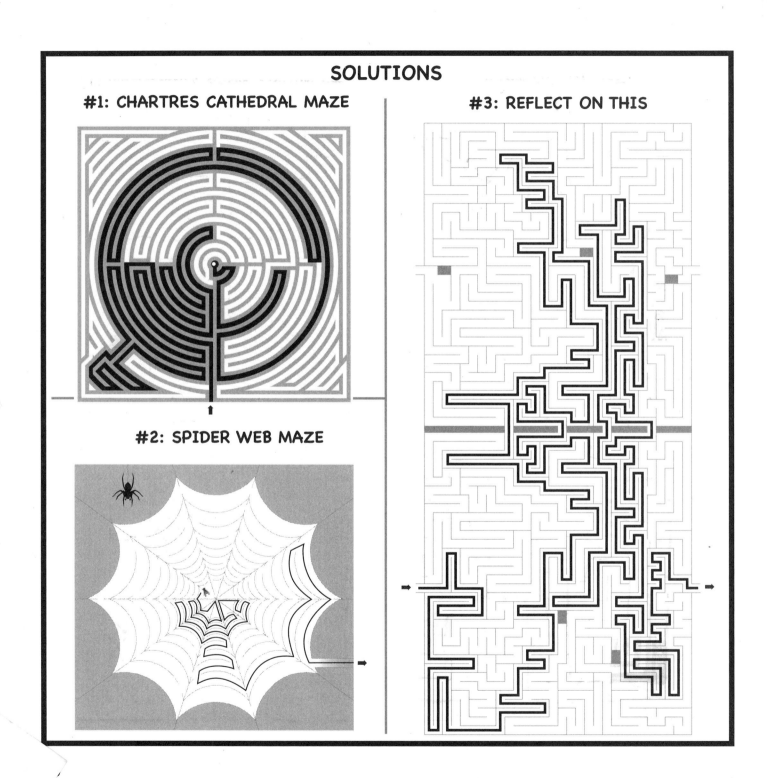

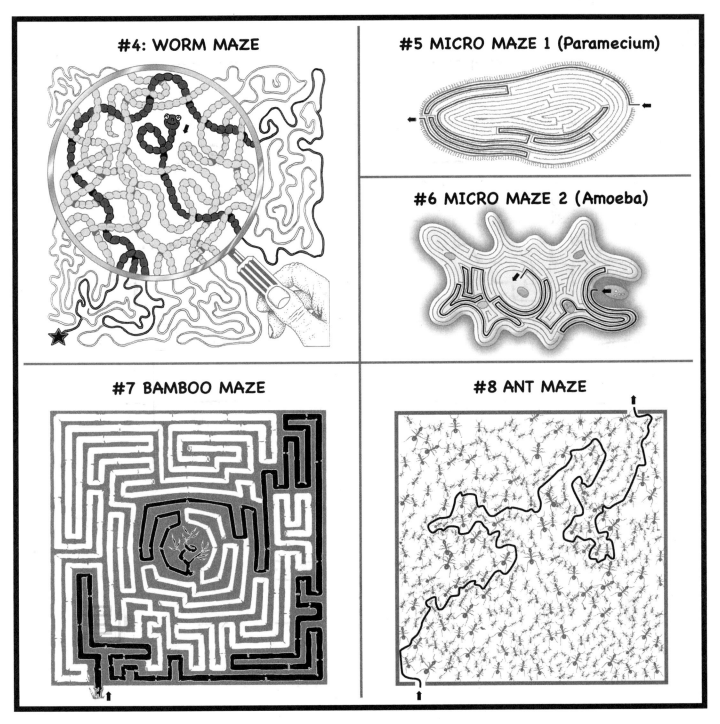

#4: WORM MAZE

#5 MICRO MAZE 1 (Paramecium)

#6 MICRO MAZE 2 (Amoeba)

#7 BAMBOO MAZE

#8 ANT MAZE

71

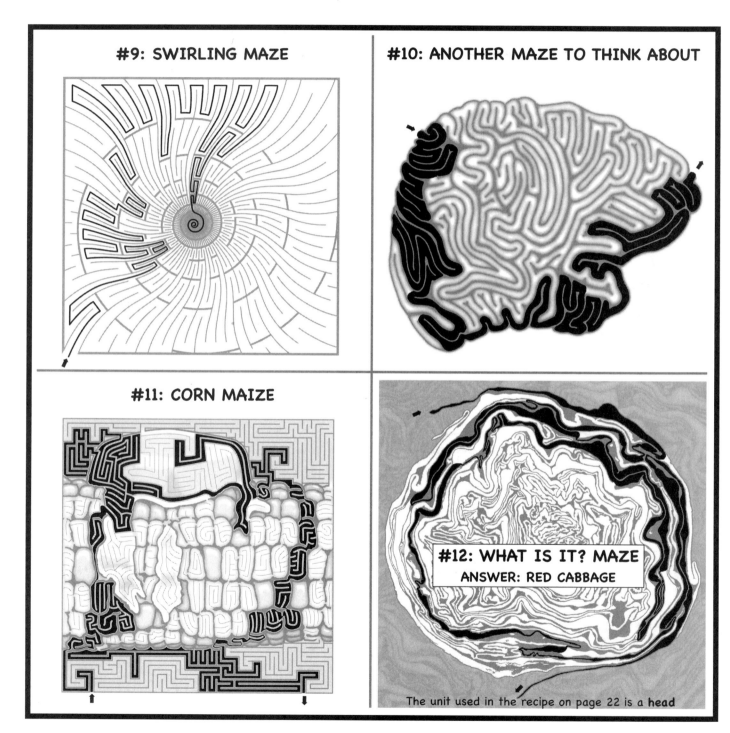

#9: SWIRLING MAZE

#10: ANOTHER MAZE TO THINK ABOUT

#11: CORN MAIZE

#12: WHAT IS IT? MAZE
ANSWER: RED CABBAGE

The unit used in the recipe on page 22 is a **head**

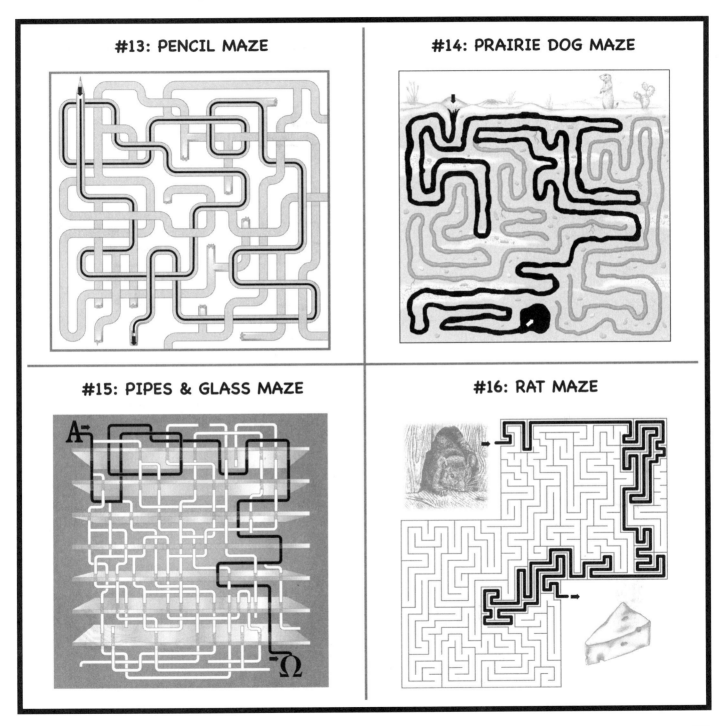

# #13: PENCIL MAZE

# #14: PRAIRIE DOG MAZE

# #15: PIPES & GLASS MAZE

# #16: RAT MAZE

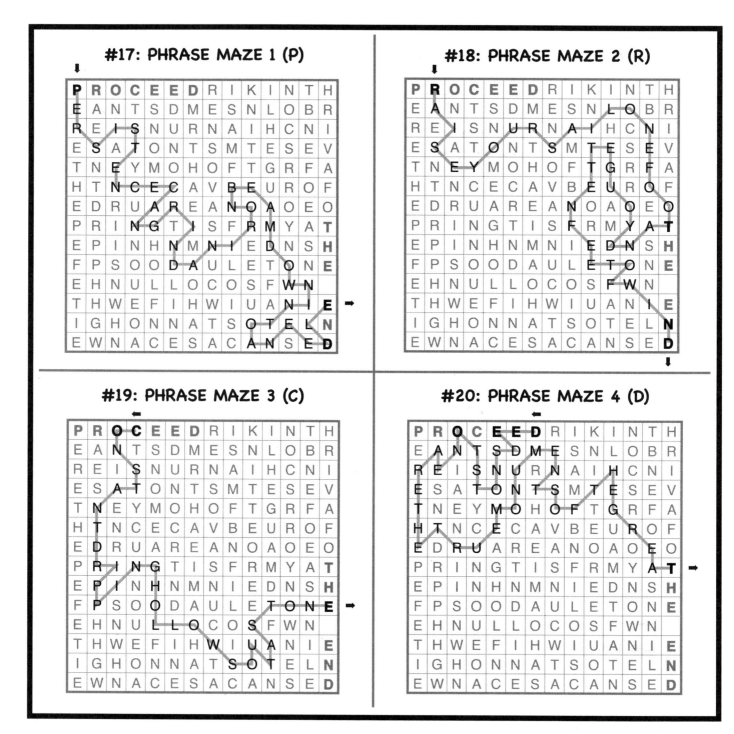

# #17: PHRASE MAZE 1 (P)

# #18: PHRASE MAZE 2 (R)

# #19: PHRASE MAZE 3 (C)

# #20: PHRASE MAZE 4 (D)

## PHRASE MAZE CLUES

**STARTING LETTER P**
Clue: Word 4 of paragraph 4 on page 32 should get you off to a good start

**STARTING LETTER R**
Clue: The first word is "RAISE"

**STARTING LETTER C**
Clue: The first word is "CONSTANT"

**STARTING LETTER D**
Clue: The first word is "DEEDS"

## PHRASE MAZE PHRASES

**STARTING LETTER D**
"DEEDS NOT STONE ARE THE TRUE MONUMENTS OF THE GREAT"
–John L. Motley

**STARTING LETTER C**
"CONSTANT DRIPPING HOLLOWS OUT A STONE"
–Lucretius

**STARTING LETTER R**
"RAISE YOUR SAIL ONE FOOT AND YOU GET TEN FEET OF WIND"
–Chinese Proverb

**STARTING LETTER P**
"PERSISTENCE CAN GRIND AN IRON BEAM DOWN INTO A NEEDLE"
–Chinese Proverb

---

## #21: BONUS PHRASE MAZE

Clue: The first word is "DREAMS"

"DREAMS HAVE AS MUCH INFLUENCE AS ACTIONS"
–Stephanie Mallarme

dreams have as much influenced actions

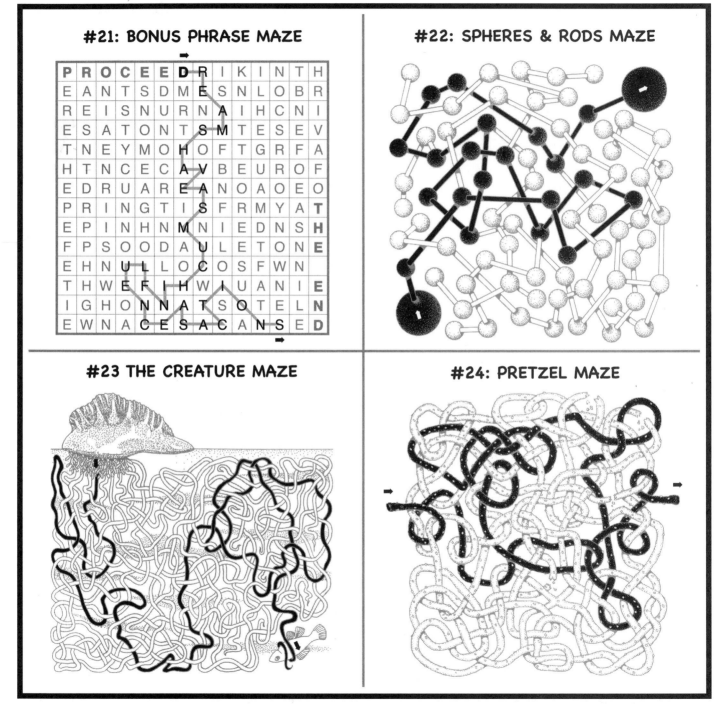

## #21: BONUS PHRASE MAZE

| P | R | O | C | E | E | D | R | I | K | I | N | T | H |
|---|---|---|---|---|---|---|---|---|---|---|---|---|---|
| E | A | N | T | S | D | M | E | S | N | L | O | B | R |
| R | E | I | S | N | U | R | N | A | I | H | C | N | I |
| E | S | A | T | O | N | T | S | M | T | E | S | E | V |
| T | N | E | Y | M | O | H | O | F | T | G | R | F | A |
| H | T | N | C | E | C | A | V | B | E | U | R | O | F |
| E | D | R | U | A | R | E | A | N | O | A | O | E | O |
| P | R | I | N | G | T | I | S | F | R | M | Y | A | T |
| E | P | I | N | H | N | M | N | I | E | D | N | S | H |
| F | P | S | O | O | D | A | U | L | E | T | O | N | E |
| E | H | N | U | L | L | O | C | O | S | F | W | N | |
| T | H | W | E | F | I | H | W | I | U | A | N | I | E |
| I | G | H | O | N | N | A | T | S | O | T | E | L | N |
| E | W | N | A | C | E | S | A | C | A | N | S | E | D |

## #22: SPHERES & RODS MAZE

## #23 THE CREATURE MAZE

## #24: PRETZEL MAZE

# #25: TREASURE MAZE

# #26: IVY MAZE

# #27: HOSE MAZE

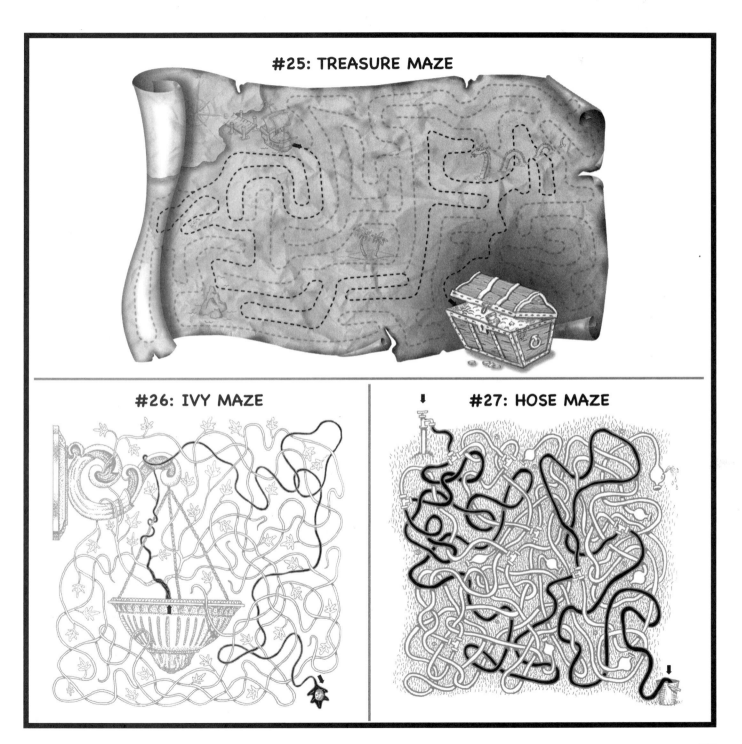

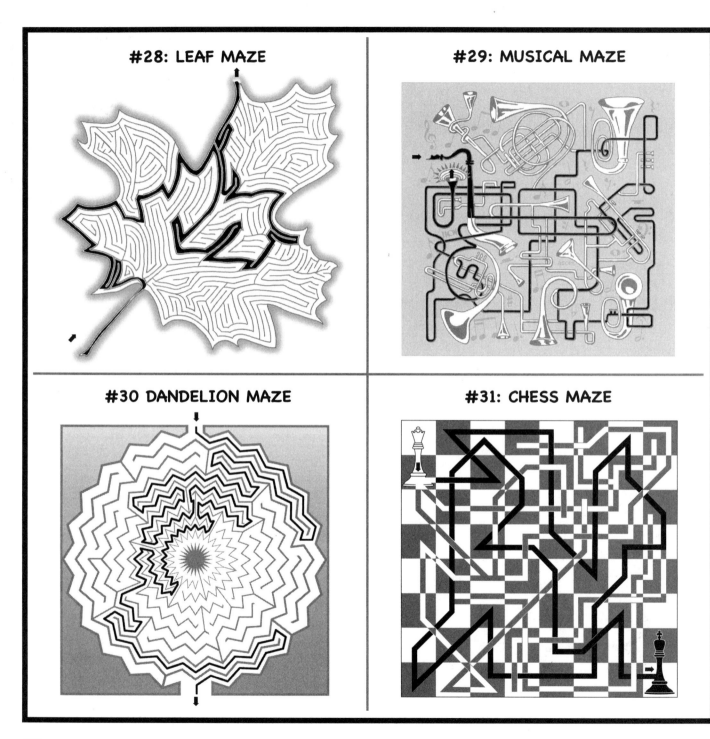

#28: LEAF MAZE

#29: MUSICAL MAZE

#30 DANDELION MAZE

#31: CHESS MAZE

## #32: GOLF MAZE

## #34: FINGERPRINT MAZE

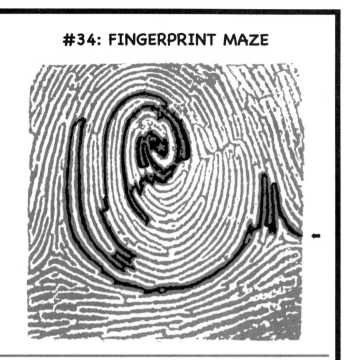

## #33: A THORNY MAZE

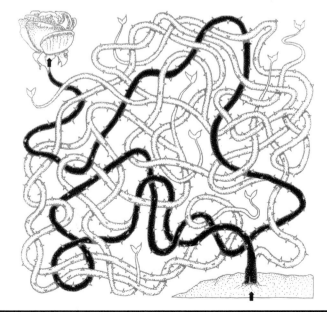

## FLOWER ANAGRAMS

Red navel = Lavender
Image run = Geranium
Even bar = Verbena
Old gas rim = Marigolds
Mantis pie = Impatiens
Ape unit = Petunia
Dodo horn nerd = Rhododendron
Angry head = Hydrangea
Sire wait = Wisteria
Grandpa son = Snapdragon
Fold if sad = Daffodils
Any hitch = Hyacinth
List up = Tulips
Nose pie = Peonies

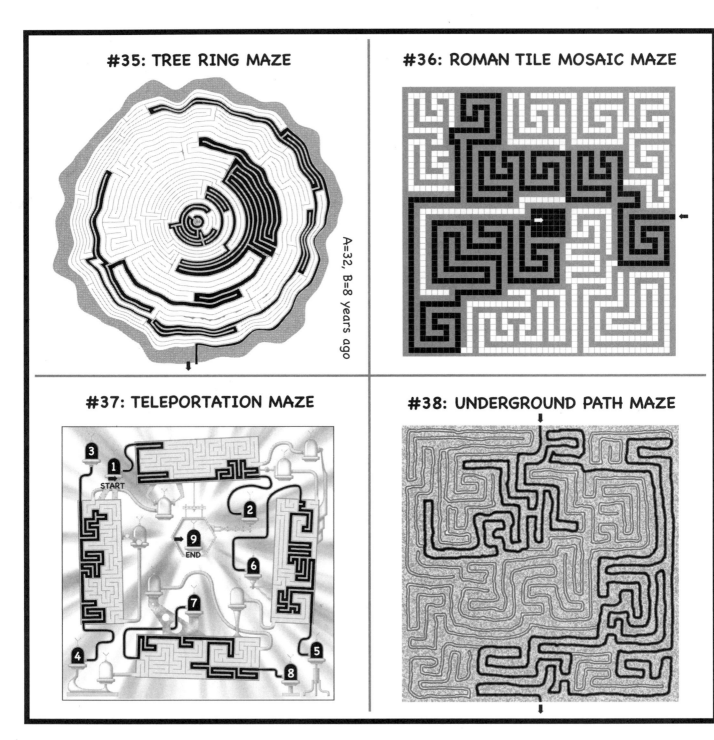

#35: TREE RING MAZE

A=32, B=8 years ago

#36: ROMAN TILE MOSAIC MAZE

#37: TELEPORTATION MAZE

#38: UNDERGROUND PATH MAZE